HORSE AND
PONY BREEDS

The new compact study guide and identifier

Caroline Ball

IDENTIFYING

HORSE AND
PONY BREEDS

The new compact study guide and identifier

Caroline Ball

CHARTWELL
BOOKS, INC.

A QUINTET BOOK

Published by Chartwell Books
A Division of Book Sales, Inc.
114, Northfield Avenue
Edison, New Jersey 08837

Reprinted 1997

This edition produced for sale
in the U.S.A., its territories
and dependencies only.

ISBN 0-7858-0051-4

This book was designed and produced by
Quintet Publishing Limited
6 Blundell Street
London N7 9BH

Creative Director: Richard Dewing
Designer: Steve Humfress
Project Editor: Katie Preston

Typeset in Great Britain by
Central Southern Typesetters, Eastbourne
Manufactured by Bright Arts (Singapore) Pte Ltd
Printed in Singapore by Star Standard Industries Pte Ltd

CONTENTS

· · · · · · · · · · · · · ·

INTRODUCTION

Horses are beautiful and complex animals. The study and development of breeds and breeding is also a complex subject and, over the years, a special vocabulary has appeared that describes the physical and mental characteristics of horses and ponies. It is essential to master this terminology to understand fully the descriptions that follow in the breed identifier.

PHYSICAL CHARACTERISTICS

UNDERSTANDING TERMS

Conformation, or the make and shape of a horse, is a very important subject for anyone interested in horses.

A horse that is *short coupled* has a shortish back, and you cannot fit more than a hand's width between its last rib and the point of its hip. This is an indication of strength and hardiness. *Slack loins* are the opposite of *short coupled,* indicating a rather long, weak back and possibly clumsy action.

Well let-down refers to the hocks, which should be "down near the ground": the lower part of the hind legs should be noticeably shorter than the upper part for more efficient leverage and less likelihood of tendon strain. The points of the hocks should be level with the front chestnuts when viewed from the sides. Similarly, the front cannons should be shorter than the forearm.

If a horse has a *deep girth,* it has plenty of depth and room for the heart and lungs. The length of the legs should not exceed the depth of the body from withers to breastbone.

If a horse's legs are too long it is said to *show a lot of daylight* – in other words, a lot of space or daylight shows beneath its body. If it's short-legged and compact, it *doesn't show much daylight* – an advantage.

Open elbows mean that you can fit your fist between the elbow and the ribcage, a great advantage which should ensure a long reach (stride) with the forelegs so that the horse *covers a lot of ground* with each stride and therefore uses less energy.

Standing over a lot of ground means that the horse appears to stand squarely with *a leg at each corner,* rather than having its legs bunched together underneath it, which is bad.

A horse described as *croup high* has the point of its croup higher than its withers. This is quite bad as the saddle will be forever sliding forwards and digging in behind the shoulders, which can make the horse very sore and injure the muscles and skin. It also gives the rider an unpleasant "going downhill" feeling. The croup should be level with the withers or slightly lower for ordinary riding.

Length of rein refers to the distance between the horse's mouth and the rider's hand. A good length here provides the security of knowing that you have *plenty in front of you,* and are not likely to go over the horse's head should he stop suddenly. Good length of rein depends on the horse having correctly proportioned neck and shoulders. If it has, it is described as *having a good front.* If not it has *poor front* or is *short in front.*

The shoulder of a riding horse should be *well sloped,* the horse being described as having *sloping shoulders.* The angle from the point of the shoulder to the point of the wither should be about 40 or 45 degrees. This angle should be the same as that formed by the pasterns and feet with the ground. The hind feet and pastern angle (called the foot/pastern axis) can be *slightly* more upright. Pasterns that are too long and sloping can be weak, upright pasterns lead to an uncomfortable ride.

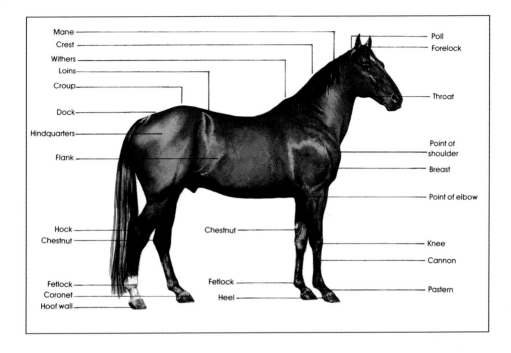

COLOURS AND MARKINGS

Coat colour and markings developed over millions of years to give the animal the best possible camouflage for the area in which it lived. The more closely it resembled its background, the less likely it was to be spotted by a predator.

One of the most primitive horse and pony colours is dun (a yellow beige) with black points (the points being mane, forelock, tail and the lower legs). In a woodland background, or on plains where by no means everything is a lush green, duns are extremely well camouflaged.

There are many old stories of good and bad colours in horses. Chestnut horses are supposedly hot tempered, black nasty tempered and lacking in stamina, bay and brown dependable, and so on. In reality colour has no bearing whatsoever on temperament or performance ability.

The only exceptions to this are horses that have pink skin under white hair. These horses are much more susceptible to the weather than others, because pink skin lacks the strengthening substance melanin which is responsible for skin and hair colour. The pink hue comes from blood circulating through colourless skin. Because this skin is less resistant to sun and wet, and hence bacteria, it becomes easily infected with skin diseases, sunburn and allergies.

The varieties of horse colours which are abundant today are the result of domesticated breeding, and bear no relation to camouflage. Some horses such as palomino, paints and pintos (piebalds, skewbalds and odd-coloured horses) are bred for special colours, and during the last century the German royal stud bred cremello (cream) horses for carriagework.

Markings are areas of white on the body, limbs and head of the horse. The terms used to describe them have been officially laid down by the various breeding authorities. On the body these are zebra marks (stripes

981299

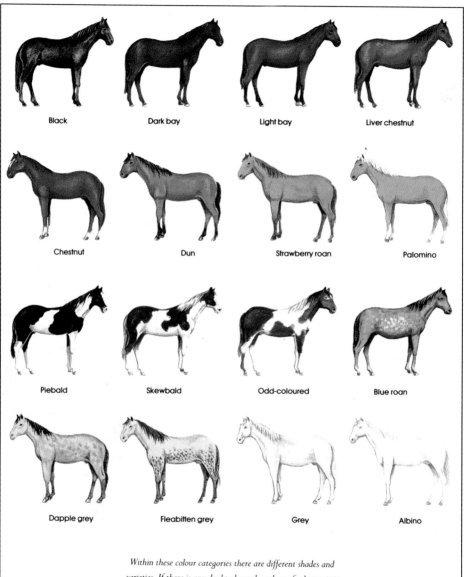

Black

Dark bay

Light bay

Liver chestnut

Chestnut

Dun

Strawberry roan

Palomino

Piebald

Skewbald

Odd-coloured

Blue roan

Dapple grey

Fleabitten grey

Grey

Albino

Within these colour categories there are different shades and varieties. If there is any doubt about the colour of a horse, it is decided by the colour of the points – the muzzle, tips of the ears, mane and tail, and lower parts of the legs.

Stripe

Blaze

White face

Snip

Star

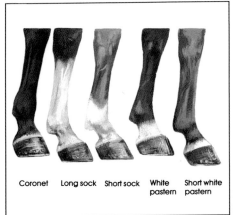

Coronet Long sock Short sock White pastern Short white pastern

On the head, markings are a star (a small white patch on the forehead); a stripe (a white line running down the face); a blaze (a broad white line from eyes to muzzle); a white face (forehead, eyes, nose and parts of the muzzle); a snip (a small white line running into or around the nostril); and wall eye (blue-white or white colouring in the eye).

Some pony breeds have a dark stripe running down the spine called a dorsal or, sometimes, an eel stripe. A few ponies and most donkeys have a further stripe running across this at the withers.

HEIGHT

The height of a horse is measured from the highest point of the withers to the ground. For accuracy, it is important that the horse is standing square on a flat surface.

On the European continent, height is measured in centimetres, while in the UK, Ireland, Australasia and North America it is measured in hands. A hand is

on the limbs, neck, withers or quarters); and whorls (patterns of hairs around a small central point). Markings on the leg are either socks (white on the fetlock and part of the cannon) or stockings (white stretching from coronet to knee or hock). Socks are always shorter than stockings.

officially defined as 4 in/10.16 cm, which is the average distance across a man's knuckles; 15 hands 2 inches, or 15.2 hands, is the accepted way of setting out a fractionalized measurement. The abbreviation *hh* stands for "hands high".

BREEDS AND TYPES

Ever since the horse first became domesticated, man has created specific breeds by selectively breeding from horses with different characteristics, to produce animals with the necessary physical and temperamental attributes to meet his own needs at the time. Many hundreds of breeds have been developed over the centuries, and they are constantly changing. Breeds die out because they are no longer needed by man. Draught and harness horses are an example of this; many of these breeds are now threatened. On the other hand, old breeds are being altered and new breeds are created, to meet new demands. The great increase in pleasure and competitive riding over the last twenty years has led to breeds being developed specifically for this.

A new breed is formally recognized when a stud book is opened. There are two types of stud book. New breeds usually have an open stud book, that is, the stallion and mare need not necessarily be of the same breed although both must be of pedigree stock. An open stud book allows for the continuing development of a breed, and for cross-breeding to correct any fault that might occur. Older breeds have a closed stud book, that is, both parents must be registered members of that breed.

CATEGORIES

Horse breeds fall into four categories: ponies, coldbloods, warmbloods and hotbloods. Pony breeds are defined as being under 14.2 hands. However there are other differences between pony and horse breeds. Many pony breeds have developed in the wild which has led to a natural cunning and hardiness that is not found in most horse breeds. They are seldom ill and

rarely go lame. They have primitive features, and most breed true to type (the breed characteristics are reproduced consistently in the offspring). The coldblood group consists of heavy work horses. They are gentle, docile, enduring and hard working. The hotblood group contains the pure bred Arab and Thoroughbred which have fiery, proud, spirited temperaments. The warmblood group is the largest today. It contains all the sports and riding horse breeds, and some of the light draught breeds. These breeds are of mixed origin. Most are descended from the Arab, but by crossing with draught or pony blood, horses have been produced that have spirit and stamina, are more robust than the Thoroughbred and Arab, and are tractable, responsive and hard-working.

There are some categories of horse that are not registered in any stud book, but that are recognized as specific types. Examples of this are the cob, the hack and the hunter (although it is possible to have a registered Thoroughbred hunter or hack).

HACK

The term hack comes from the word hackney or haquenai, which in medieval times referred to a hired horse of poor quality. Gradually the term came to refer to a general riding horse as opposed to a horse bred for hunting.

Today hack refers to a top-quality riding horse for people who like to ride out and look good. As well as having good manners and appearance, it must be well behaved, have a good action, respond well to the aids, and have the ability to jump small fences. In Europe, a small Thoroughbred type with a dash of Arab is popular as a hack, whereas in the USA the Saddlebred is favoured.

HUNTER

The term hunter refers to a horse that is suited to carrying a rider safely, sensibly and comfortably behind foxhounds for a season's hunting.

Different types of hunting country require different types of horse. In flattish country with large, open

HACK

HUNTER

fields and big fences, speed and bold jumping are essential, and Thoroughbred or near-Thoroughbred types are best. In rough or hilly country, or where the going is heavy, and where the scent is less good, crosses of Thoroughbred and light draught or native pony breeds are better. They provide a mount with a calm temperament, surefootedness, lots of stamina and a good instinct for self-preservation.

RIDING PONY

The riding pony type has been developed to provide a mount that is particularly suitable for children. Native breeds that evolved in the wild have many valuable qualities; they are intelligent, hardy and surefooted. However, pure-bred native ponies do not necessarily provide the best type of pony for children, since they are broad in the back and can be very strong-willed. It has been the policy in many countries for some time now to cross native breeds with Arab or Thorough-

bred blood, to produce ponies that have good conformation, athleticism, elegance and gentleness in addition to the character and sturdiness of the native pony.

COB

The term cob refers to a distinct type of strong, stocky horse. Only the Welsh Cob is classified as a breed. They are the result of crosses such as a heavyweight hunter mare with a Thoroughbred stallion, or a Welsh Cob mare with a Thoroughbred riding pony or even an Arab stallion.

Cobs are compact and sturdy, obedient and placid, and provide a very comfortable ride without too much speed. They are ideal for elderly or nervous riders, and for those who particularly need a horse with a calm temperament such as race-horse trainers supervising a string of young Thoroughbreds. Cobs are also immensely strong and can carry a heavy rider all day in the hunting field.

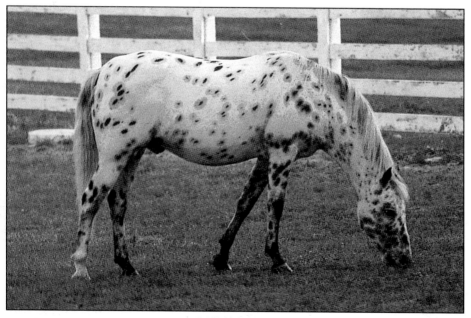

RIDING PONY

COB

COUNTRIES OF ORIGIN

NO PARTICULAR COUNTRY OF ORIGIN

NORTH AMERICA

SOUTH AMERICA

BRITAIN AND IRELAND

WESTERN EUROPE

SCANDINAVIA

SOUTHERN EUROPE

EASTERN EUROPE

MIDDLE EAST AND AFRICA

FAR EAST AND AUSTRALASIA

HOW TO USE THIS BOOK

Although many breeds of horse and pony originated in a specific place or small region, they have now become widely dispersed around the world. They are listed here according to their country of origin. All the current major horse and pony breeds are included, and many less well-known ones are listed with their major founding breed. Information is given on the origins of each breed, the uses that they have been put to over the centuries and what they are best suited for today. The development of each breed is described and ancestry charts summarize the development of each breed by listing in chronological order the breeds that have contributed to it from its beginnings up until the twentieth century. The key information is shown clearly under the following subheadings: Origin, Height, Physique, Features, Character, Principal Uses. In addition, the category of each horse (page 10) – coldblood, warmblood, hotblood, pony – is shown under the breed name.

NO SPECIFIC COUNTRY OF ORIGIN

ARAB
THOROUGHBRED

The Arab is the oldest pure-bred horse in the world. Evidence suggests that it evolved from prehistoric wild horses that spread across Asia to the Middle East. The Arab was captured and domesticated in several countries and this has produced several strains, the most famous being the Bedouin Arab. The Arab is very popular for founding and refining other breeds due to its ability to breed true to type, and consequently it has had more influence on the world's horse population than any other breed.

ORIGIN Arabia
COLOUR chestnut, bay, grey
HEIGHT 14.3 hands
PHYSIQUE small head, "dished" face, crested neck, long sloping shoulder, short back, deep girth, strong hindquarters, tail carried high and arched, hard clean leg, short cannon bone

FEATURES fast free-floating action, stamina and toughness
CHARACTER brave, intelligent, fiery, enduring
PRINCIPAL USES riding, improving other breeds

ANCESTRY

ASIATIC
WILD STOCK

THOROUGHBRED
THOROUGHBRED

The Thoroughbred is the race-horse *par excellence*. It is the fastest, and most valuable, horse in the world. The breed was developed in England in the seventeenth century by crossing the fastest native mares with imported breeds. The importance of the pedigree (and track-record) of thoroughbreds can be traced to the time of the first General Stud Book (1791) when all the horses listed were descended from just three Arab stallions.

ORIGIN UK
COLOUR solid colours
HEIGHT 16 hands
PHYSIQUE varies from close-coupled sprinters with large, powerful hindquarters to big-framed, longer backed, big-boned chasers. Must have an elegant head, long neck, sloping shoulder, prominent wither and silky coat.
FEATURES fast and active
CHARACTER bold, brave and spirited
PRINCIPAL USES racing, riding, cross-breeding

ANCESTRY

ARAB

TURK

BARB

GALLOWAY

QUARTER-HORSE
WARMBLOOD

Named after the quarter-mile race at which it proved so successful in seventeenth century Virginia and the Carolinas, the Quarter-Horse came to be valued for its versatility, strength and endurance: it proved to be an ideal ranch horse as the West was opened up. Today it is the most numerous breed in the USA, with 2 million registered there. A further 800,000 are registered worldwide. The Quarter-Horse is the fastest horse in the world over a quarter-mile (0.4 km), the current record being around 20 seconds.

ANCESTRY

ARAB

BARB

TURK

ANDALUSIAN

THOROUGHBRED

ORIGIN USA
COLOUR solid colours, usually chestnut
HEIGHT 14.3–15.1 hands
PHYSIQUE short head, muscular neck, short-coupled body, broad powerful hindquarters, fine legs.

FEATURES fast and versatile
CHARACTER intelligent, sensible, active and nimble
PRINCIPAL USES riding, ranchwork, rodeos, racing

MUSTANG
WARMBLOOD

North America's feral horse (the continent had no indigenous horses), the Mustang is descended from the horses of Spanish settlers, but has been wild for over 300 years. It has contributed to the development of many American breeds, including the Quarter-Horse, the Appaloosa and the Pinto, but the wild Mustang has declined in numbers and is now protected by law.

ANCESTRY

ANDALUSIAN

ARAB

BARB

TURK

ORIGIN western states of America and Mexico
COLOUR all colours
HEIGHT 14–15 hands
PHYSIQUE lightweight but sturdy build, tough legs and feet
FEATURES hardy and frugal

CHARACTER independent, intractable
PRINCIPAL USES riding, especially endurance riding, stockwork

APPALOOSA
WARMBLOOD

Originally bred by the Nez Percé Indians, the Appaloosa is recognized to have six distinct patterns of spots, although no two horses are exactly the same: Leopard (white with dark spots); Snowflake (dark with white spots); Spotted Blanket (mainly dark with dark spots on white back or hindquarters; White Blanket (the reverse of Spotted Blanket); Marble (dark coat at birth, fading almost to white); Frost Tip (mostly dark with light spots on loins and hips).

ORIGIN western USA

COLOUR six basic patterns of spots, usually on roan or white

HEIGHT 14.2–15.2 hands

PHYSIQUE short-coupled, thin mane and tail, hard feet which are often striped

FEATURES striking appearance

CHARACTER courageous, docile

PRINCIPAL USES riding, cow pony, parade and circus horse

ANCESTRY

ANDALUSIAN

ARAB

BARB

TURK

MORGAN
WARMBLOOD

An old-established breed named after Justin Morgan of Vermont, one of the owners of the original stallion, Figure. It excelled at both saddle and harness racing and at pulling heavy weights, and even today the Morgan is the only breed that has to be shown as a harness, show and draught horse. During the nineteenth century the Morgan was used in the foundation of other great American breeds, including the Standardbred, the Saddlebred and the Tennessee Walking Horse.

ORIGIN Massachusetts, USA
COLOUR predominantly bay, also brown, black and chestnut
HEIGHT 14—15 hands
PHYSIQUE slightly concave face, thick neck, deep chest, broad back, muscular quarters and high-set, full tail; legs set square
FEATURES versatile and tough, with an elegant high action

CHARACTER good-natured, hard-working and active
PRINCIPAL USES riding, driving, draught

ANCESTRY

WELSH COB

THOROUGHBRED

NATIVE STOCK

SADDLEBRED
WARMBLOOD

An elegant, high-stepping horse which was developed in the nineteenth century by plantation owners who wanted a comfortable but stylish and eye-catching mount. In addition to its natural gaits, it has two man-made gaits: the slow gait, a slow four-beat movement, and the rack, a snappy knee and hock action with which it can reach speeds of 30 mph (50 km/h).

ORIGIN USA
COLOUR black, brown, bay, grey, chestnut
HEIGHT 15—16 hands
PHYSIQUE narrow, refined head held high, large eyes, long elegant neck and sloping shoulders, short body, strong flexible hindquarters, long fine legs, tail held very high
FEATURES unusual gaits
CHARACTER intelligent and gentle, sweet-tempered
PRINCIPAL USES riding, driving, showing

ANCESTRY

THOROUGHBRED

MORGAN

NARRANGANSETT PACER

STANDARDBRED
WARMBLOOD

The fastest harness-racing horse in the world, the Standardbred was developed in the eighteenth century and almost all can be traced back to four stallions sired by the exceptional Thoroughbred trotter called Messenger. Its name comes from the standard for trotting which was laid down by the American Trotting Register in 1879. Trotters had to attain a time of 2 minutes 30 seconds over 1 mile (1.6 km) and pacers a time of 2 minutes 25 seconds.

ANCESTRY

THOROUGHBRED

CANADIAN TROTTER

HACKNEY

NARRANGANSETT PACER

ARAB

BARB

MORGAN

ORIGIN USA
COLOUR any solid colour
HEIGHT 14–16 hands
PHYSIQUE usually Thoroughbred-type, but more muscular with longer back, short legs and powerful shoulders
FEATURES stamina, speed
CHARACTER courageous and active, but calm
PRINCIPAL USES racing, driving

TENNESSEE WALKING HORSE
WARMBLOOD

The Tennessee Walking Horse, or Walker, has a walk, which is a smooth gliding action, a canter and a running walk – a unique, smooth movement even up to 15 mph (24 km/h) which cannot be taught to any other breed. In the canter it elevates its forehand with a rolling motion while its hindquarters remain almost level. The running walk is now inbred; foals are seen performing it just by copying their dams.

ANCESTRY

THOROUGHBRED

NARRANGANSETT PACER

MORGAN

STANDARDBRED

SADDLEBRED

ORIGIN Tennessee, USA
COLOUR chestnut, black, bay roan; white markings common
HEIGHT 15–16 hands
PHYSIQUE straight profile, long powerful neck and sloping shoulders, broad chest, short back, strong sloping hindquartrs, fine legs, full tail carried very high
FEATURES unique action, now inbred
CHARACTER docile and willing, alert
PRINCIPAL USES riding, showing

PALOMINO
WARMBLOOD

Unlike most breeds, the Palomino is defined by colour rather than conformation, and it does not breed true. Only in the USA is it recognized as a breed; elsewhere it is registered as a type. The early emperors of China are reputed to have ridden these golden horses, but today's Palominos developed from horses arriving with Spanish settlers which then bred with mild mustangs.

ORIGIN California, USA
COLOUR gold, with light mane and tail, white markings on legs permitted
HEIGHT usually over 14 hands
PHYSIQUE variable, but of riding horse type
FEATURES distinctive coloration
CHARACTER variable, but usually intelligent and a good general-purpose horse
PRINCIPAL USES riding, including trekking, ranchwork, rodeos

ANCESTRY

MUSTANG

PINTO
WARMBLOOD

The colourful horse traditionally associated with the American Indians, the Pinto can be of many different types. It is primarily defined by its distinctive patchy coat, but three American registers cover Pinto categories: the American Paint Horse Registry, the Pinto Registry and the Moroccan Spotted Horse Association.

ORIGIN USA
COLOUR Overo (large bold patches of black with white); Tobiano (white with smaller patches of any colour except black)
HEIGHT variable
PHYSIQUE variable: can be of several categories, including Stock, Saddle, Hunter and gaited types
FEATURES variable
CHARACTER variable (see above), but usually intelligent and enduring
PRINCIPAL USES ranchwork, riding, showing

ANCESTRY

MUSTANG

PONY OF THE AMERICAS
PONY

The first pony breed to have been developed in the USA. Although only dating from the 1950s, it has proved extremely popular for trail riding, jumping and racing, particularly among young riders.

ORIGIN USA

COLOUR Appaloosa colours and patterns

HEIGHT 11.2–13.2 hands

PHYSIQUE Arab-type head, good shoulders, deep chest, short back, rounded body and strong hindquarters, clean legs

FEATURES action: smooth and free

CHARACTER willing and gentle, versatile

PRINCIPAL USES children's riding pony

ANCESTRY

SHETLAND PONY

APPALOOSA

CANADIAN CUTTING HORSE
WARMBLOOD

This has still not been recognized as a distinct breed, only as a type, but is a popular choice for working with cattle being, like the Quarter-Horse, extremely strong, fast and agile.

ORIGIN Canada

COLOUR any

HEIGHT 15.2–16.1 hands

PHYSIQUE similar to American Quarter-Horse: long body, short legs with powerful hindquarters

FEATURES fast and agile

CHARACTER intelligent, easy to break

PRINCIPAL USES ranchwork

ANCESTRY

EUROPEAN STOCK

QUARTER-HORSE

CRIOLLO
WARMBLOOD

This agile, intelligent horse is the favourite cattle horse of Argentinian gauchos. Generations of exposure to the tough conditions of the pampas have made it exceptionally hardy and today the best animals from which to breed are chosen by an annual ride of 470 miles (750 km), carrying 238 lb (108 kg), during which they may not be fed. Argentinian polo ponies are Criollo/Thoroughbred crosses.

ORIGIN Argentina
COLOUR dun with dark points and dorsal stripes; sometimes roan, chestnut or bay
HEIGHT 14 hands
PHYSIQUE short broad head, muscular neck and strong shoulders, broad chest, deep body on fine strong legs with small feet
FEATURES tough and manoeuvrable

CHARACTER willing, with great powers of endurance
PRINCIPAL USES riding, stockwork

ANCESTRY

ANDALUSIAN

BARB

ARAB

PERUVIAN STEPPING HORSE
WARMBLOOD

One of several South American Paso breeds, which have in common the *paso* gait – a lateral four-beat stride which produces a smooth, ambling pace that can be sustained over a long period. The Peruvian has great stamina, developed from working in the high Andes. It is gaining popularity around the world due to its comfortable, easy gait and excellent temperament.

ORIGIN Peru
COLOUR bay, chestnut, brown, black, grey
HEIGHT 14.2−15.2 hands
PHYSIQUE long crested neck with head held high, deep broad chest and body on fine strong legs, full mane and tail
FEATURES endurance and a special extended gait, similar to an amble

CHARACTER docile, with great powers of endurance
PRINCIPAL USES riding, stockwork

ANCESTRY

ANDALUSIAN

BARB

SPANISH JENNET

SOUTH AMERICA

FALABELLA
PONY

The world's smallest horse reaches a height of only 34 in (86 cm), the size of a large dog. It is treasured as a miniature carriage horse and as a pet.

ORIGIN Argentina
COLOUR all colours
HEIGHT under 7 hands
PHYSIQUE proportioned like a miniature horse, with fine bones and small feet
FEATURES hardy; the smallest pony in the world
CHARACTER gentle, friendly and courageous
PRINCIPAL USES harness pony, pet

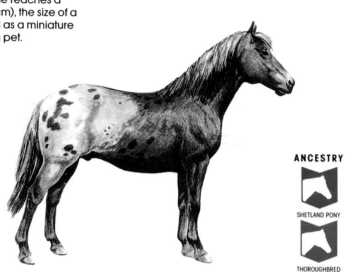

ANCESTRY

SHETLAND PONY

THOROUGHBRED

PASO FINO
WARMBLOOD

The distinctive *paso* gaits of this breed are the *paso fino*, at the pace of a slow walk, the *paso corto* at trotting speed, and the *paso largo*, performed at a slow canter.

ORIGIN Puerto Rico
COLOUR all colours
HEIGHT 14.3 hands
PHYSIQUE Arab-type head, strong back and quarters, hard fine legs
FEATURES extra four-beat gait
CHARACTER spirited yet tractable
PRINCIPAL USES riding, stockwork

ANCESTRY

ANDALUSIAN

BARB

SPANISH JENNET

GALICENO
PONY

The Galiceno's name reflects its origins in the ponies of Galicia, northern Spain. It has become very popular in the USA since its introduction there in 1959. The Arab (in its Garrano blood) has given it intelligence and stamina despite its delicate frame.

ORIGIN Mexico
COLOUR bay, black, dun, sorrel, grey
HEIGHT 12–13.2 hands
PHYSIQUE intelligent head, straight shoulders and narrow chest, short back, fine legs with small feet
FEATURES versatile, and a natural running walk
CHARACTER alert, kind and very intelligent
PRINCIPAL USES transport, ranchwork

ANCESTRY

GARRANO

MANGALARGA
WARMBLOOD

The Brazilian Mangalarga, developed about 100 years ago, is an excellent riding horse, its *marcha* gait providing a comfortable rocking ride. The heavier Campolino is very similar.

ORIGIN Minas Gerais, Brazil
COLOUR bay, chestnut, roan, grey
HEIGHT 15 hands
PHYSIQUE longish head, short back, powerful hindquarters and long legs, low-set tail
FEATURES hardy; individual gait called the *marcha*, between a canter and a trot
CHARACTER hardy, with good powers of endurance
PRINCIPAL USES riding, stockwork

ANCESTRY

CRIOLLO

ANDALUSIAN

ALTÉR REAL

BRITAIN AND IRELAND

DARTMOOR
PONY

The Dartmoor, once used by miners to carry tin down from the moors, is hardy and surefooted, and its build and temperament make it particularly suitable for a child's first pony. It is also valued for cross-breeding.

ORIGIN Dartmoor (Devon), England

COLOUR bay, brown, black

HEIGHT up to 12.2 hands

PHYSIQUE small head with very small ears, strong neck, shoulders set well back, strong hindquarters and slim hard legs, high-set full tail

FEATURES surefooted and tough; long-lived

CHARACTER quiet, reliable, kind and sensible

PRINCIPAL USES riding

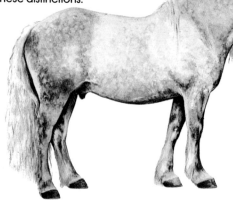

ANCESTRY

CELTIC PONY

HIGHLAND
PONY

The Highland was originally divided into two strains: the Garron from the mainland (at 14.2 hands the largest and strongest native breed) and the smaller Western Isles strain. Cross-breeding has now more or less eliminated these distinctions.

ORIGIN Western Isles and mainland, Scotland

COLOUR dun, ranging from golden-blue to silver-blue, with dorsal stripe; sometimes black, grey-black or brown

HEIGHT 13—14.2 hands

PHYSIQUE neat head with short ears, solid deep body, short strong legs with feathers and well-shaped hard hooves, full mane and tail

FEATURES strong but not fast

CHARACTER docile, sensitive and responsive; trusting

PRINCIPAL USES riding, trekking, deer-stalking

ANCESTRY

CELTIC PONY

GALLOWAY

ARAB

FELL
PONY

The Fell pony, from the western side of the Pennines, is renowned for its strength – when used for carting lead, it was reputed to have carried daily loads of 220 lb (100 kg) 30 miles (50 km).

ORIGIN Cumbria, England
COLOUR usually black, also brown, bay, grey; white markings on legs permitted
HEIGHT 13–14 hands
PHYSIQUE alert head on long neck, muscular body, strong legs with feathering, long thick mane and tail
FEATURES strong, with great stamina; a fast trotter
CHARACTER lively and alert, a hard worker
PRINCIPAL USES riding, driving, trekking

ANCESTRY

CELTIC PONY

GALLOWAY

FRIESIAN

DALES
PONY

A close relation of the Fell, it was also employed for farmwork and carting, but with the advent of mechanization its numbers dropped dramatically and by the 1950s it was in danger of becoming extinct.

ORIGIN Eastern Pennines, England
COLOUR black or brown; white star permitted
HEIGHT 13.2–14.2 hands
PHYSIQUE neat head on strong neck, powerful compact body, short legs, thick mane and tail, and feathering on feet
FEATURES strong, surefooted
CHARACTER sensible, quiet, hard-working
PRINCIPAL USES riding, trekking, agricultural work

ANCESTRY

CELTIC PONY

FRIESIAN

GALLOWAY

WELSH COB

EXMOOR
PONY

The tough little Exmoor is thought to have existed in prehistoric times and, due to the moor's isolation, has changed little from its early ancestors. Exmoors still run wild, enduring bitter conditions without human help. Once a year they are rounded up for branding and registration. Although seemingly intractable, they make good children's ponies once trained, and are strong enough to carry adults.

ANCESTRY

CELTIC PONY

ORIGIN Exmoor (Somerset and Devon), England
COLOUR bay, brown or mouse dun with mealy muzzle; must not include white
HEIGHT up to 12.2 hands (mares); up to 12.3 hands (stallions and geldings)
PHYSIQUE broad forehead, thick neck and deep chest, short clean legs with hard feet, prominent eyes, thick springy coat
FEATURES strong and enduring
CHARACTER intelligent, quick-witted and kind
PRINCIPAL USES riding, cross-breeding

NEW FOREST
PONY

The origins of the New Forest pony are probably similar to those of the Exmoor and Dartmoor, and they may all have come from one massive area of forest thought to have covered southern England. Herds of ponies still run wild in the New Forest but, being less isolated than other native types, have long been used to human contact and are friendly and docile. Since the nineteenth century attempts have been made to ensure the quality of the breed by introducing stallions of other breeds, such as Thoroughbreds, to breed with the native mares.

ORIGIN New Forest (Hampshire), England
COLOUR any colour except piebald or skewbald; white markings permitted
HEIGHT 12−14.2 hands
PHYSIQUE large head, long sloping shoulders, short back with deep girth, hard legs and good feet

FEATURES hardy and frugal
CHARACTER willing, very friendly and docile, very quick to learn
PRINCIPAL USES children's riding pony

ANCESTRY

CELTIC PONY

NATIVE BREEDS

THOROUGHBRED

ARAB

BRITAIN AND IRELAND

CONNEMARA
PONY

Ireland's only native pony is a pretty, oriental-looking breed; one theory is that it was crossed with Spanish Jennets shipwrecked during the Spanish Armada in 1588.

ORIGIN Co. Connaught, Ireland

COLOUR usually grey but can be black, brown or bay

HEIGHT 13–14 hands

PHYSIQUE intelligent-looking, well carried head, medium-length neck on sloping shoulders, deep compact body on short legs

FEATURES hard and surefooted, a good jumper

CHARACTER intelligent, kind, sensible and tractable

PRINCIPAL USES riding, jumping, driving

ANCESTRY

CELTIC PONY

SPANISH JENNET

ARAB

THOROUGHBRED

SHETLAND
PONY

For nearly 2,000 years the Shetland Isles were the only home for this, the smallest of Britain's native breeds. But in the nineteenth century it was exported and bred in great numbers to serve as a pit pony on the mainland.

CHARACTER courageous and independent, headstrong but gentle

PRINCIPAL USES riding, driving, pet

ORIGIN Shetland and Orkney Islands, UK

COLOUR black, bay, brown, chestnut, grey or part-colours

HEIGHT up to 10.2 hands

PHYSIQUE small head on sloping shoulders, deep thick-set body, short back, short legs with some feathering and small open feet

FEATURES hardy and strong; can pull loads twice own weight

ANCESTRY

CELTIC PONY

*I*RISH DRAUGHT
COLDBLOOD/WARMBLOOD

The number of pure-bred horses has declined since the agricultural recession in the late nineteenth century but the Irish Government and the Irish Draught Horse Society are working to restore the breed.

ORIGIN Ireland

COLOUR bay, brown, chestnut, grey

HEIGHT 15–17 hands

PHYSIQUE intelligent-looking head on short muscular neck, long powerful body, strong legs with little feathering, large round feet

FEATURES good jumper

CHARACTER quiet and sensible, willing, alert

PRINCIPAL USES hunting, cross-breeding for competition horses

ANCESTRY

NATIVE STOCK

CONNEMARA

THOROUGHBRED

*I*RISH HALF-BRED
WARMBLOOD

Only recently classified as a separate breed, the Irish Half-Bred is still being developed. It produces outstanding show-jumpers and eventers.

ORIGIN Ireland

COLOUR any solid colour

HEIGHT 16.1 hands

PHYSIQUE variable: either classic hunting or show-jumping type

FEATURES strong and athletic

CHARACTER intelligent and bold, sensible

PRINCIPAL USES hunting, show-jumping, eventing

ANCESTRY

IRISH DRAUGHT

THOROUGHBRED

CONNEMARA

The native ponies of Wales are considered by many to be the prettiest of the British pony breeds. The Welsh Pony stud book is divided into four sections, A, B, C and D. The Celtic Pony and the Arab produced the Welsh Mountain Pony (section A), which was in turn crossed with a small Thoroughbred descendant of the Darley Arabian, called Merlin, to produce the Welsh Pony or Merlin (section B). The Welsh Mountain Pony crossed with Spanish horses and perhaps the now extinct Old Welsh Carthorse produced the Welsh Cob (section D), of which the Welsh Pony (section C) is a smaller version.

WELSH MOUNTAIN PONY (SECTION A)

PONY

ORIGIN Wales

COLOUR any colour except piebald or skewbald

HEIGHT up to 12 hands

PHYSIQUE small head with concave face, crested neck and sloping shoulders, short back, short legs and neat feet, high-set tail

FEATURES very enduring

CHARACTER intelligent, kind, brave and spirited

PRINCIPAL USES riding, breeding

ANCESTRY

CELTIC PONY

ARAB

34

WELSH PONY
(SECTION B)

PONY

ORIGIN Wales
COLOUR any colour except piebald or skewbald
HEIGHT up to 13.2 hands
PHYSIQUE similar to Welsh Mountain, but taller and more lightly built
FEATURES very enduring, good action
CHARACTER intelligent, kind, brave and spirited
PRINCIPAL USES riding

WELSH COB
(SECTION D)

WARMBLOOD

The Welsh Pony (section C) is a smaller version of the Welsh Cob.

ORIGIN Wales
COLOUR any solid colour
HEIGHT 14–15.1 hands
PHYSIQUE compact and of great substance, good head on strong shoulders, deep powerful back, silky feathers
FEATURES strong and with great stamina; a high knee action
CHARACTER bold and energetic, intelligent and equable temper
PRINCIPAL USES riding, driving

ANCESTRY

ORIENTAL

WELSH PONY

TROTTER

ANCESTRY

WELSH MOUNTAIN PONY

WELSH COB

THOROUGHBRED
(Merlin, a small stallion, direct descendant of the Darley Arabian)

SHIRE
COLDBLOOD

Despite the lack of demand for the Shire as a working draught horse, its popularity as a show horse has not waned; its enormous size and weight provide a perennial crowd-puller.

ANCESTRY

FRIESIAN

OLD ENGLISH BLACK HORSE

FLANDERS HORSE

NATIVE STOCK

ORIGIN Midland counties, England
COLOUR black, bay or grey, with white markings
HEIGHT 16–18 hands
PHYSIQUE slightly convex profile, wide chest and deep broad girth, dense muscular body, long legs and abundant feathering
FEATURES strong; tallest breed in the world
CHARACTER docile, gentle, kind, hard-working
PRINCIPAL USES draught, showing

HACKNEY
WARMBLOOD/PONY

Developed from regional trotting breeds, the Hackney was specifically bred in the nineteenth century to produce an elegant fast means of transport on the expanding network of proper roads.

ANCESTRY

NORFOLK ROADSTER

THOROUGHBRED

ORIGIN UK
COLOUR bay, dark brown, black
HEIGHT up to 14 hands (pony); 14–15.3 hands (horse)
PHYSIQUE small head with convex face, long neck, compact body with deep chest, short legs with strong hocks, fine silky coat, high-set tail carried high
FEATURES high stepping action
CHARACTER spirited and alert, courageous
PRINCIPAL USES driving

SUFFOLK PUNCH
COLDBLOOD

In earlier times the Suffolk was considered the best horse for heavy agricultural work: it is long-lived, often working well into its twenties, has tremendous pulling power, and can thrive on poor keep despite its size.

ORIGIN East Anglia, England

COLOUR chestnut in seven shades (red, gold, copper, yellow, liver, light or dark)

HEIGHT 16 hands

PHYSIQUE large head on deep neck, massive shoulders, round compact body, lean legs with short cannon bone

FEATURES strong, with good action; long-lived

CHARACTER docile but active, intelligent

PRINCIPAL USES draught, showing

ANCESTRY

NATIVE GREAT HORSE

FLANDERS HORSE

NORFOLK TROTTER

COB

THOROUGHBRED

CLEVELAND BAY
WARMBLOOD

Probably the oldest of the British horse breeds, the Cleveland Bay was developed in the north-east as a packhorse: its immediate ancestor was the horse used by medieval travelling merchants or "chapmen" in northern England.

ORIGIN Yorkshire, England

COLOUR bay; small star permitted

HEIGHT 15.2–16 hands

PHYSIQUE large head on long neck, long deep-girthed body on short strong clean legs

FEATURES strong and versatile; long-lived

CHARACTER intelligent, sensible, calm, tractable

PRINCIPAL USES driving, riding

ANCESTRY

NATIVE CHAPMEN HORSE

THOROUGHBRED

CAMARGUE
PONY

Known as the White Horse of the Sea, the Camargue is an ancient breed which still runs wild in the marshlands of the Rhône delta, France. Once caught and broken they are popular with *gardiens*, the local cowboys, for rounding up the equally famous black bulls of the area. The Camargue has been recognized as a breed since 1968. Annual round-ups and selective gelding help control and improve the quality of the breed.

ORIGIN The Camargue, southern France

COLOUR grey; foals are born dark and whiteness increases with age

HEIGHT 13.2–14.2 hands

PHYSIQUE large Oriental-type head with straight profile, short shoulders and back, slight hindquarters, fine legs with large feet

FEATURES hardy

CHARACTER tractable and reliable once tamed

PRINCIPAL USES herding, trekking

ANCESTRY

ANCIENT NATIVE BREED

ARAB

BARB

TRAKEHNER
WARMBLOOD

The Trakehnen Stud, established in 1732, was in what was once East Prussia (now called Poland) and they developed the Trakehner using the local Schwieken horse. In the winter following the end of World War II, about 700 Trakehners trekked west with refugees fleeing the Russians. These horses were used to re-establish the breed in Germany, while the Trakehners remaining behind were used to create the Polish Wielkopolski.

ANCESTRY

SCHWIEKEN

ARAB

THOROUGHBRED

ORIGIN Poland/Germany
COLOUR any solid colour, usually dark
HEIGHT 16–16.2 hands
PHYSIQUE elegant head and long neck, prominent withers, deep chest, strong back with rounded hindquarters, slender legs and good feet
FEATURES elegant, good-looking, with extravagant action

CHARACTER spirited and courageous, versatile and tractable
PRINCIPAL USES riding, competition

39

BELGIAN HEAVY DRAUGHT
COLDBLOOD

One of the strongest of the heavy breeds, the Belgian is thought to be a direct descendant of the Flanders War Horse. The traditional workhorse on farms in Belgium, it has also been used to found or improve other breeds of heavy horse such as the Rhineland and the Ardennes. Its alternative name is the Brabant, after the region around Brussels from which it originates.

ORIGIN Brabant, Belgium

COLOUR mostly red roan with black points; sometimes bay, brown, dun or grey

HEIGHT 16 hands

PHYSIQUE square, relatively small head on strong deep neck, powerful shoulders, short compact body with massive powerful hindquarters, short strong legs with some feathering

FEATURES strong, with a good action and great presence

CHARACTER docile, willing, yet active and bold

PRINCIPAL USES draught

ANCESTRY

FLANDERS HORSE

PERCHERON
COLDBLOOD

The most famous of the French draught horses originated in the Paris basin area of La Perche, and was first bred to carry heavy-armoured knights into battle. Further breeding produced a very strong working horse with, thanks to its Arab blood, more elegance than most. The Boulonnais, also from northern France, is very similar, as is the slightly smaller Postier Percheron.

ORIGIN France
COLOUR grey or black
HEIGHT 15.2–17 hands
PHYSIQUE straight profile, deep crest beck, deep powerful chest, short body, very powerful hindquarters, thick muscular legs with very little feathering, full mane and tail.

FEATURES great presence and good action
CHARACTER active, intelligent and good-natured
PRINCIPAL USES draught

ANCESTRY

ORIENTAL

HEAVY DRAUGHT
BREEDS

NORMAN

FRIESIAN
WARMBLOOD

One of the oldest European horse breeds, the Friesian's origins are unknown. It was popular with the Romans, and a heavy ancester is known to have lived in the Friesland region over 3,000 years ago. The modern Friesian's outstanding feature is its fast, high trot, making it popular as competition and show horse, and in the circus ring.

ANCESTRY

FRIESLAND STOCK

ANDALUSIAN

ARAB

BARB

OLDENBURG

ORIGIN Friesland, Netherlands
COLOUR black
HEIGHT 15 hands
PHYSIQUE fine long head on crested neck, strong compact body, rounded hindquarters, short legs with feathering, full mane and tail

FEATURES great presence
CHARACTER quiet, willing, sensitive and hard-working
PRINCIPAL USES driving, riding, all-round workhorse

FRENCH TROTTER
WARMBLOOD

The first trotting course in France opened at Cherbourg in 1836 and precipitated a demand for good horses. Early horses were usually a Norfolk Trotter/Anglo-Norman cross and later introductions, including the American Standardbred.

ORIGIN Calvados (Normandy), France

COLOUR usually chestnut, bay or brown

HEIGHT 16.1 hands

PHYSIQUE alert head on strong straight shoulders, short back, well-muscled powerful hindquarters, long hard legs with short cannon bone

FEATURES athletic and fast

CHARACTER willing and tough, with competitive spirit

PRINCIPAL USES trotting, riding, cross-breeding

ANCESTRY

NORFOLK TROTTER

NATIVE STOCK

STANDARDBRED

ANGLO-ARAB
WARMBLOOD

It is the French who have developed the Anglo-Arab as a distinct breed. It excels as a competition horse, and is also used to improve the quality of other breeds such as the Selle Française.

ORIGIN UK, France, Poland

COLOUR most solid colours

HEIGHT 16 hands

PHYSIQUE delicate head, withers set well back, deep chest, short back and well-proportioned hindquarters, long slender legs, high-set tail

FEATURES stamina and good movement

CHARACTER brave, spirited and intelligent, with good temper

PRINCIPAL USES riding, racing, competition

ANCESTRY

ORIENTAL

ARAB

THOROUGHBRED

43

HANOVERIAN
WARMBLOOD

The breed was founded in 1735 at the Celle State Stud. Over the centuries the Hanoverian has changed considerably to suit different requirements. The horse bred for agricultural and carriage work was later adapted to the needs of the army and then, after World War I, further developed for farming and riding. Since World War II the aim of its breeders has been a world-class competition horse, a role in which it now excels.

ANCESTRY

GREAT WAR HORSE

HOLSTEIN

THOROUGHBRED

CLEVELAND BAY

ANDALUSIAN

TRAKEHNER

ARAB

ORIGIN Hanover and Lower Saxony, Germany
COLOUR all solid colours
HEIGHT 15.3–17 hands
PHYSIQUE variable, but a compact powerful body on short strong legs
FEATURES athletic

CHARACTER intelligent, sensible, willing and bold
PRINCIPAL USES riding, competition

LIPIZZANER
WARMBLOOD

The Lipizzaner is one of the world's most famous breeds, thanks to the Spanish Riding School of Vienna and its prodigious displays of high-school dressage. Such displays were popular in the European courts in the sixteenth century, and Archduke Charles of Austria imported Andalusian stallions, recognized as the premier dressage horses, to cross with local mares at the Lipizza Stud.

ANCESTRY

ARAB

BARB

ANDALUSIAN

NEOPOLITAN

KLADRUBER

FREDERICKSBORG

ORIGIN Austria

COLOUR grey (born dark, but lightening as they mature)

HEIGHT 15–16 hands

PHYSIQUE largish head with straight profile and small ears, crested neck, compact body, powerful rounded hindquarters and strong clean legs

FEATURES athletic, late to mature

CHARACTER intelligent, obedient and willing

PRINCIPAL USES high-school dressage, driving

*D*RAUGHT BRETON
COLDBLOOD

In the nineteenth century the tough Draught Breton was crossed with the Norfolk Trotter and Hackney to create a lighter, more elegant horse with a smart action – the Postier. The two types of Breton now have their own divisions within one stud book.

ANCESTRY

NATIVE STOCK

PERCHERON

ARDENNES

BOULONNAIS

ORIGIN France
COLOUR grey, chestnut, bay
HEIGHT 15–16 hands (Draught); up to 15 hands (Postier)
PHYSIQUE wide short head on strong neck, broad body, short muscular legs with a little feathering. Postier lighter and more elegant
FEATURES strong and active (Draught less energetic)

CHARACTER lively, intelligent and good-natured
PRINCIPAL USES light draught, agricultural work

FRANCHES MONTAGNES
WARMBLOOD

The Franches Montagnes, also known as the Freiburger, is invaluable in its native Switzerland where it is still used on the fields that are too steep for a tractor; the Swiss Army also depend on it for transporting men and equipment through the mountains. Its breeding, controlled by the state-financed National Stud at Avenches, concentrates on character and ability rather than conformation.

ANCESTRY

NORMAN

ANGLO-NORMAN

THOROUGHBRED

DRAUGHT BREEDS

ORIGIN Jura, Switzerland
COLOUR most solid colours
HEIGHT 14.3–15.2 hands
PHYSIQUE small head on compact body, strong legs with a little feathering, but conformation can vary
FEATURES strong, with good stamina, surefooted
CHARACTER active, hard-working, docile

PRINCIPAL USES agricultural work

OLDENBURG
WARMBLOOD

The Oldenburg has been bred in the
north-west of Germany since the
seventeenth century, but over the years
has become a lighter and more refined
horse, pre-eminently suited to riding.

ANCESTRY

FRIESIAN

ANDALUSIAN

BARB

HANOVERIAN

CLEVELAND BAY

THOROUGHBRED

ANGLO-NORMAN

ORIGIN Oldenburg and East
Friesland, Germany
COLOUR any solid colour,
usually black, brown or bay
HEIGHT 16.2–17.2 hands
PHYSIQUE straight profile,
strong neck and muscular
chest and body, strong
hindquarters, short legs
FEATURES matures early
CHARACTER bold, sensible
PRINCIPAL USES riding,
competition, driving

EAST FRIESIAN
WARMBLOOD

Until the 1940s the East Friesian developed alongside the Oldenburg, the two breeds constantly being exchanged and interbred. Since then the East Friesian has been further bred with Arabs and Hanoverians to produce a lighter, more compact horse.

ORIGIN eastern Germany
COLOUR any solid colour
HEIGHT 15.2–16.2 hands
PHYSIQUE similar to the Oldenburg from which it was developed, but with a lighter frame and more elegant head
FEATURES good temperament
CHARACTER bold, spirited and good-natured
PRINCIPAL USES riding, driving

ANCESTRY

OLDENBURG

ARAB

HANOVERIAN

HAFLINGER
PONY

All members of the Haflinger breed can be traced back to an Arab stallion, El Bedavi XXII, bred with native ponies in the Austrian Tyrol. His son, 249 Folie, gave the breed its distinctive colouring.

ORIGIN Austrian Tyrol
COLOUR chestnut with flaxen mane and tail
HEIGHT 14 hands
PHYSIQUE medium-sized head with pointed muzzle, strong neck, deep girth, long broad back, well-muscled hindquarters and short legs
FEATURES frugal, tough and surefooted, long-lived
CHARACTER hard-working, good-tempered and docile
PRINCIPAL USES mountain pony, driving, packhorse, riding

ANCESTRY

NATIVE MOUNTAIN STOCK

ARAB

49

HOLSTEIN
WARMBLOOD

The Holstein is known to have lived in the marshlands of Schleswig-Holstein as early as the fourteenth century, and was originally a heavy, powerful horse. Since the nineteenth century it has been successively bred with lighter, more refined breeds.

ANCESTRY

MARSH HORSE

ANDALUSIAN

NEAPOLITAN

CLEVELAND BAY

THOROUGHBRED

ORIGIN Emsburg, Holstein, Germany
COLOUR most solid colours
HEIGHT 16–17 hands
PHYSIQUE elegant head on strong neck, powerful shoulders, deep girth, compact body with strong hindquarters and short legs
FEATURES good action

CHARACTER intelligent, willing and bold, versatile and good-natured
PRINCIPAL USES riding, competition

SCHLESWIG HEAVY DRAUGHT
COLDBLOOD

The Schleswig was developed during the nineteenth century specifically to meet the demand for horses capable of heavy agricultural work, and its blood includes that of other heavy horses including the Jutland, a Danish war-horse believed to have been ridden by the Vikings.

ANCESTRY

JUTLAND

SUFFOLK PUNCH

BOULONNAIS

BRETON

ORIGIN Germany
COLOUR usually chestnut with flaxen mane and tail
HEIGHT 15.1–16 hands
PHYSIQUE large head with convex profile, short powerful neck, deep girth, long flat body on short muscular legs with a little feathering

FEATURES active, good action
CHARACTER willing and kind
PRINCIPAL USES draught

GELDERLAND
WARMBLOOD

Originally created as a versatile farm horse suitable for draught and riding, the Gelderland has been carefully developed in the course of the twentieth century into a first-class carriage horse.

ANCESTRY

NATIVE STOCK

ANDALUSIAN

NORFOLK TROTTER

OLDENBURG

ANGLO-NORMAN

EAST FRIESIAN

HACKNEY

ORIGIN Gelder, Netherlands
COLOUR solid colours, usually chestnut or grey
HEIGHT 15.2–16 hands
PHYSIQUE plain head with convex profile, strong arched neck and deep shoulders, compact body, powerful hindquarters and short legs, high-set tail
FEATURES extravagant action and great presence

CHARACTER quiet and good-natured, active
PRINCIPAL USES riding, driving, carriage horse

SWEDISH ARDENNES
COLDBLOOD

Very similar to the Belgian Ardennes which is one of its forebears, the Swedish Ardennes has declined in numbers since the demand for heavy agricultural horses has all but gone, although it is still used for hauling timber in inaccessible mountain areas.

ORIGIN Sweden

COLOUR black, brown, bay or chestnut

HEIGHT 15.2–16 hands

PHYSIQUE small head on crested neck, immensely muscular compact body on short legs with little feathering

FEATURES frugal, and very strong, eager worker

CHARACTER kind and gentle, energetic

PRINCIPAL USES draught

ANCESTRY

ARDENNES

SWEDISH HORSE

KNABSTRUP
WARMBLOOD

This heavy spotted horse dates back to the time of the Napoleonic wars, when a spotted mare of Spanish origins with the unlikely name of Flaebehoppen was crossed with a palomino Fredericksborg stallion. As with the Appaloosa, no two horses have exactly the same patterning.

ORIGIN Denmark

COLOUR spotted: Appaloosa patterns on roan base

HEIGHT 15.3 hands

PHYSIQUE conformation varies – similar to Fredericksborg, but lighter build

FEATURES active; bred mainly for distinctive pattern

CHARACTER intelligent and tractable

PRINCIPAL USES riding, circus

ANCESTRY

SPANISH BLOOD

FREDERICKSBORG

SWEDISH HALF-BRED
WARMBLOOD

Also known as the Swedish Warmblood, the Half-Bred was developed some 300 years ago as a cavalry horse. Since the stud book was opened in 1894 the breed has been constantly tested for conformation, character and performance. It is now in demand all over the world, especially for show-jumping, eventing and dressage.

ANCESTRY

ARAB

BARB

ANDALUSIAN

FRIESIAN

NATIVE STOCK

THOROUGHBRED

TRAKEHNER

HANOVERIAN

ORIGIN Sweden
COLOUR any solid colour
HEIGHT 15.2—16.3 hands
PHYSIQUE small head with elegant features, strong deep shoulders, deep body with straight back, rounded hindquarters, fine legs with short cannon bones
FEATURES extravagant, straight action

CHARACTER intelligent and sensible, obedient, bold
PRINCIPAL USES riding, driving, competition

FJORD
PONY

Little cross-breeding has occurred to change this ancient and primitive breed; it closely resembles the Asiatic wild horse depicted in prehistoric cave paintings. The pony ridden by the Vikings is still much used in mountain areas for farmwork and in harness, and is popular as a children's pony and in competition driving.

ORIGIN Norway

COLOUR yellow or mouse dun with pronounced dorsal stripe, silver and black mane and tail

HEIGHT 13–14.2 hands

PHYSIQUE concave profile, short neck merging into shoulder without definition, powerful body, short legs with some feathering, coarse upright mane

FEATURES surefooted, very hardy

CHARACTER gentle, strong-willed and hard-working, tractable

PRINCIPAL USES farmwork, driving, mountain work, packhorse, children's pony

ANCESTRY

ASIATIC WILD HORSE

DØLE
WARMBLOOD

The most widespread of the Norwegian breeds, the Døle accounts for about two-thirds of the Norwegian horse population. Variations had been adapted for different purposes. The Døle Trotter, a fast harness horse, is now used for racing.

ORIGIN Norway
COLOUR solid colours, usually black, brown or bay
HEIGHT 14.2–15.2 hands
PHYSIQUE varies from draught type to lighter pony build: small head on crested neck, strong shoulders, deep girth, powerful hindquarters, short legs with moderate feathering
FEATURES tough and versatile
CHARACTER adaptable and patient
PRINCIPAL USES riding, driving, light draught

ANCESTRY

NATIVE STOCK

THOROUGHBRED

DANISH DRAUGHT BREEDS

FREDERICKSBORG
WARMBLOOD

For 200 years Denmark's Royal Fredericksborg Stud, founded in 1562, supplied their top riding horse to all the courts of Europe, but by 1839 the Stud had been closed. The breed was registered again in 1923, but the horses are still not numerous.

ORIGIN Denmark
COLOUR usually chestnut
HEIGHT 15.2–16 hands
PHYSIQUE large plain head on strong neck, powerful shoulders, deep chest, long strong body, straight croup, strong legs
FEATURES strong and active, good in harness
CHARACTER good-tempered and tractable
PRINCIPAL USES riding, driving

ANCESTRY

ANDALUSIAN

NEAPOLITAN

FINNISH COLDBLOOD

The Finns have always bred horses on the basis of performance rather than looks, and the Finnish has a heavier and a lighter version, and a trotter bred for racing. All are known for their speed, stamina and agility.

ORIGIN Finland

COLOUR chestnut, bay, brown or black

HEIGHT 15.2 hands

PHYSIQUE short neck, upright shoulders, deep chest, long back and strong hindquarters, strong legs with light feathering

FEATURES tough and fast, long-lived

CHARACTER quiet and tractable, lively, intelligent

PRINCIPAL USES farmwork, riding, trotting

ANCESTRY

NATIVE FOREST PONIES

FINNISH DRAUGHT

ICELANDIC PONY

There are several variations of Icelandic Pony, but they all have great stamina, strength and surefootedness. Their unusual gaits are the ample, a running walk, and the *tölt*, a rapid amble much valued for crossing steep icy terrain.

ORIGIN Iceland

COLOUR most colours

HEIGHT 12–13 hands

PHYSIQUE large head on strong short neck, deep compact body on strong clean legs with large feet, thick mane and tail

FEATURES tough, able to amble

CHARACTER docile, friendly and independent

PRINCIPAL USES farmwork, packhorse, draught, mining

ANCESTRY

FJORD

CELTIC PONY

LUSITANO
WARMBLOOD

Although once primarily used as a cavalry horse and chosen by farmers for its strength, the Lusitano is above all known as the mount of Portuguese bull-fighters, renowned for its agility, speed, obedience and courage.

ORIGIN southern and central Portugal

COLOUR usually grey, but can be any solid colour

HEIGHT 15–16 hands

PHYSIQUE small head with small ears and a straight profile, muscular neck, compact body, powerful hindquarters, long fine legs, abundant mane and tail

FEATURES frugal and hardy

CHARACTER intelligent, responsive and very brave

PRINCIPAL USES riding, bull-fighting

ANCESTRY

ANDALUSIAN

ARAB

ITALIAN HEAVY DRAUGHT
COLDBLOOD

The energy and willingness to work of this distinctively coloured large horse made it indispensible to Italian farmers before mechanization, but its numbers are now much reduced.

ORIGIN northern and central Italy

COLOUR liver chestnut with flaxen mane and tail

HEIGHT 15–16 hands

PHYSIQUE fine long head on short crested neck, powerful shoulders, deep broad chest, robust body with broad flat back, round hindquarters and muscular legs with some feathering

FEATURES fast and strong

CHARACTER active, willing, kind and docile

PRINCIPAL USES farmwork, meat

ANCESTRY

BRETON

SKYROS
PONY

The smallest and best known of Greece's indigénous breeds is the Skyros. On its native island it is used as a packhorse and for light farmwork, but on the mainland it is most often a children's pony.

ORIGIN Skyros, Greece
COLOUR dun, brown or grey
HEIGHT 9.1–11 hands
PHYSIQUE small head and ears, short neck, upright shoulders, narrow body, long legs with tendency towards cow hocks
FEATURES best-known of Greece's native ponies
CHARACTER hard-working
PRINCIPAL USES packhorse, farmwork, children's pony

ANCESTRY

TARPAN

BOSNIAN
PONY

A descendant of the wild Tarpan of eastern Europe, the Bosnian is a native of the mountainous areas of Bosnia and Herzegovina, but is much used all over the region as a working pony and for riding.

ORIGIN Bosnia and Herzegovina
COLOUR dun, brown, chestnut, grey or black
HEIGHT 12.2–15 hands
PHYSIQUE compact mountain pony, thick mane and tail
FEATURES tough and enduring
CHARACTER intelligent
PRINCIPAL USES packhorse, farmwork

ANCESTRY

TARPAN

ARAB

SOUTHERN EUROPE

ANDALUSIAN
WARMBLOOD

The elegant Andalusian, which excels in high-school work, was used to found many other breeds, including the Lipizzaner of Austria, and its blood is found in the "dancing" horses of the Americas, such as the Peruvian Stepping Horse and Paso Fino. Saved from the ravages of Napoleon's Peninsular campaign by the Carthusian monks in Jerez, who successfully founded a new stud, it is today much sought-after and admired.

ANCESTRY

NATIVE STOCK

BARB

ARAB

ORIGIN Andalusia, Spain
COLOUR usually grey
HEIGHT 15.2–16 hands
PHYSIQUE broad forehead, large eyes and convex profile, long arched neck, deep short body, powerful rounded hindquarters,
strong legs with short cannon bone, luxuriant mane and tail
FEATURES agile and athletic with an elegant springy action, great presence
CHARACTER docile, willing, proud and affectionate
PRINCIPAL USES high-school dressage, parades, bull-fighting

ALTÉR REAL
WARMBLOOD

The national horse of Portugal is closely related to its neighbour, the Andalusian, and was bred from them during the eighteenth century for the fashionable high-school dressage demonstrations. After suffering a downturn in fortunes due to war, cross-breeding and changing fashion, the Altér is once again showing its quality and popularity.

ORIGIN Portugal
COLOUR bay, brown or grey
HEIGHT 15–16 hands
PHYSIQUE convex profile, strong shoulders, deep broad chest, short body, powerful hindquarters and hard legs with flexible hocks

FEATURES elegant and powerful, with high-stepping action
CHARACTER intelligent, temperamental and brave
PRINCIPAL USES riding, high-school dressage

ANCESTRY

ANDALUSIAN

SALERNO
WARMBLOOD

Horse-breeding has long been important in Italy. The now extinct Neapolitan is in the blood of many of the world's modern breeds, and was one of the main lines used to develop the Salerno during the sixteenth century, since when it has been a popular riding horse. In turn the Salerno has provided the parentage for the new Italian Saddle-Horse.

ORIGIN Meremma and Salerno, Italy

COLOUR any solid colour

HEIGHT 16 hands

PHYSIQUE large refined head, good shoulders, prominent withers, strong sloping hindquarters and short legs

FEATURES aristocratic, top-class riding horse

CHARACTER intelligent, responsive

PRINCIPAL USES riding, cross-breeding

ANCESTRY

NEAPOLITAN

ANDALUSIAN

TARPAN
PONY

The wild Tarpan, closely resembling the wild horses of the Ice Age, was almost hunted to extinction before the end of the eighteenth century (Tarpan meat was considered a delicacy). However the breed has been "re-created" using close descendants and domesticated Tarpan-types and a closely studied herd now roams wild in Poland's Popielno Forest.

ORIGIN Poland

COLOUR mouse to brown with dorsal stripe, dark mane and tail. Zebra stripes may appear on forelegs and inner thighs. Coat may change to white in winter

HEIGHT 13 hands

PHYSIQUE long broad head on short thick neck, sloping shoulders, long back, thin hindquarters, fine legs

FEATURES tough and fertile

CHARACTER intractable and tenacious

PRINCIPAL USES zoo exhibit

ANCESTRY

MONGOLIAN WILD HORSE

ASIATIC WILD HORSE

EASTERN EUROPE AND CENTRAL ASIA

WIELKOPOLSKI
WARMBLOOD

When a contingent of the Trakehnen Stud trekked west at the end of World War II, those left became the foundation stock for the Masuren and the Poznan, which were then combined to form the Wielkopolski.

ANCESTRY

TRAKEHNER

HANOVERIAN

THOROUGHBRED

KONIK

POZNAN

MASUREN

EAST PRUSSIAN

ORIGIN Poland
COLOUR usually chestnut or bay
HEIGHT 16 hands
PHYSIQUE small head on strong neck, deep girth, medium-length back, good hindquarters and fine legs

FEATURES carefully bred as all-rounder
CHARACTER gentle, intelligent and active
PRINCIPAL USES riding, light farmwork

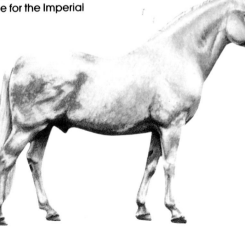

SHAGYA ARAB
WARMBLOOD

Named after the grey Arab which sired the breed, the Shagya was developed by crossing Arabs and native stock to produce a robust cavalry mount and light carriage horse.

ORIGIN Hungary
COLOUR usually grey
HEIGHT 15 hands
PHYSIQUE Arab-type but slightly more robust
FEATURES hardy, frugal and active
CHARACTER intelligent, good-natured, enduring
PRINCIPAL USES riding, driving, cavalry

ANCESTRY

SYRIAN ARAB

KLADRUBER
WARMBLOOD

At the oldest operational stud in the world (founded by the Emperor Maximilian II in 1597), the Kladruber was bred as a ceremonial coach horse for the Imperial court.

ORIGIN Kladruby, Czech Republic
COLOUR grey (from the Kladruby stud) or black (from the Slatinany stud)
HEIGHT 16—17 hands
PHYSIQUE Andalusian type but with larger convex profile, strong arched neck, long body and rounded hindquarters
FEATURES superb carriage horse
CHARACTER proud, obedient, intelligent and good-tempered
PRINCIPAL USES driving, riding

ANCESTRY

ANDALUSIAN

ANGLO-NORMAN

HANOVERIAN

OLDENBURG

ORLOV TROTTER
WARMBLOOD

The Orlov Trotter is probably the best known of the "Russian" horse breeds. It was developed in the eighteenth century when trotting races were very popular. During the nineteenth century the Orlov, bred by Count Alexius Orlov, was the best trotting horse in the world, but later lost its supremacy to the American Standard-bred. It has more recently been crossed with the Standardbred to produce the Russian Trotter.

ANCESTRY

DANISH BLOOD

ARAB

DUTCH BLOOD

THOROUGHBRED

MECKLENBURG

NORFOLK TROTTER

ORIGIN Russia
COLOUR usually grey or black
HEIGHT 15.2–17 hands
PHYSIQUE small head on long neck, upright shoulders, broad chest, deep girth, long straight back, powerful loins and muscular hindquarters, fine hard legs with some feathering
FEATURES active and fast
CHARACTER active, bold
PRINCIPAL USES trotting, driving, riding

AKHAL TEKÉ
WARMBLOOD

The nomadic Turkmen tribes of central Asia rode the Akhal Teké into battle, and its extraordinary powers of endurance and frugal requirements made it ideally equipped for desert life, qualities it has not lost. In 1935 a group of Akhal Tekés trekked 2,672 miles (4,300 km) to Moscow, a journey which included crossing 225 miles (360 km) of desert in three days without water. The closely related Iomud is more compact and not so fast.

ANCESTRY

TURKOMAN

ORIGIN Russia
COLOUR usually bay or chestnut with metallic bloom
HEIGHT 14.2–15.2 hands
PHYSIQUE small elegant head on long thin neck, high sloping shoulder, long back, shallow body on long legs, low-set tail, sparse mane and tail
FEATURES great powers of endurance, magnificent movement
CHARACTER bold and courageous, but obstinate and temperamental, difficult to handle
PRINCIPAL USES riding, competition

67

DON
WARMBLOOD

As the mount of the Cossacks, the Don proved its endurance against the invading Napoleonic forces during the infamous winter of 1812. The breed was improved during the nineteenth century by infusions of Turkoman, Karabakh and Karabir blood, and the Don in turn has been used to improve other Russian breeds such as the Bashkersky (used for pulling sleighs), the Kazakh pony and the Budyonny, for which it provided the foundation stock.

ANCESTRY

TURKOMAN

KARABAKH

KARABIR

THOROUGHBRED

ORLOV TROTTER

ORIGIN Russian steppes
COLOUR usually chestnut, bay or grey
HEIGHT 15.2–16.2 hands
PHYSIQUE wide-set eyes, long neck, long broad back, strong hindquarters and long hard legs

FEATURES versatile, frugal and with great stamina
CHARACTER calm and reliable
PRINCIPAL USES riding, long-distance riding/racing

VLADIMIR HEAVY DRAUGHT
COLDBLOOD

The Vladimir has enormous strength, carefully bred into it since its foundation towards the end of the nineteenth century. It was developed from British and French heavy horses.

ANCESTRY

CLEVELAND BAY

SUFFOLK PUNCH

SHIRE

ARDENNES

PERCHERON

ORIGIN Vladimir, Russia
COLOUR any solid colour, but bay most common
HEIGHT 16 hands
PHYSIQUE small head on long strong neck, powerful shoulders, broad body with stout hindquarters, strong legs with feathering
FEATURES active and powerful
CHARACTER docile, good-tempered, active
PRINCIPAL USES draught

KARABAKH
WARMBLOOD

Going back to the fifth century, the Karabakh has Turkoman, Persian and Arab blood and was particularly popular in the eighteenth century. There are no pure-bred Karabakhs left today.

ANCESTRY

PERSIAN

TURKOMAN

ARAB

ORIGIN Karabakh mountains, Azerbaidzhan
COLOUR dun, bay or chestnut with metallic sheen
HEIGHT 14.2 hands
PHYSIQUE small fine head on strong neck, prominent withers, strong compact body with powerful hindquarters, fine legs and good feet, low-set tail
FEATURES energetic and tough, surefooted
CHARACTER calm and robust, quick-witted
PRINCIPAL USES riding, racing

FURIOSO
WARMBLOOD

One of Hungary's high-quality half-breds, the Furioso excels as a harness horse and is much in demand all over the world for competition driving. A Furioso/North Star cross, the Mozohegyes, is fast being looked on as Hungary's top sports horse.

ORIGIN Hungary
COLOUR dark, often with white markings
HEIGHT 16 hands
PHYSIQUE long, strong neck and powerful shoulders, strong back, powerful hindquarters, low-set tail
FEATURES robust
CHARACTER intelligent and tractable
PRINCIPAL USES riding, driving, competition, steeple-chasing

ANCESTRY

THOROUGHBRED

ARAB

NATIVE STOCK

MURAKOSI
COLDBLOOD

Until World War II the Murakosi, Hungary's strong and energetic draught horse, was immensely popular, but due to decimation during the war and the decline in demand, its numbers are now much reduced.

ANCESTRY

ORIGIN Hungary
COLOUR chestnut with flaxen mane and tail
HEIGHT 16 hands
PHYSIQUE large head with convex profile, strong frame with pronounced dip in back, powerful hindquarters and muscular legs with light feathering
FEATURES strong and active
CHARACTER kind, willing and docile
PRINCIPAL USES draught, farmwork

NATIVE STOCK

ARDENNES

PERCHERON

NORIKER

HUNGARIAN HALF-BRED

BUDYONNY
WARMBLOOD

The Budyonny was created at the army stud at Rostov by Marshal Budyonny. The highly selective breeding produced a fast, enduring horse for riding or harness work which, recrossed with Thoroughbred blood, now excels at equestrian competition.

ORIGIN Russia
COLOUR chestnut or bay with golden sheen
HEIGHT 15.2–16 hands
PHYSIQUE small head on strong neck, long sloping shoulders, strong compact body, long rounded croup, fine hard legs, low-set tail
FEATURES fast and enduring
CHARACTER calm and good-natured, intelligent
PRINCIPAL USES riding, competition, steeple-chasing

ANCESTRY

THOROUGHBRED

DON

KAZAKH

TERSKY
WARMBLOOD

The gentle, athletic Tersky was originally bred for steeple-chasing, but it is usually now raced on the flat against other Arabs. Its natural grace has also made it a popular choice for dressage and the circus ring.

ORIGIN Stavropol, Caucasus, Russia
COLOUR usually grey, but can be bay
HEIGHT 15 hands
PHYSIQUE straight profile, deep chest, muscular hindquarters, fine hard legs, high-set tail
FEATURES fast, enduring and beautiful
CHARACTER gentle and intelligent
PRINCIPAL USES flat-racing, competition, circus

ANCESTRY

STRELETSK ARAB

KABARDIN

DON ARAB

SHAGYA ARAB

THOROUGHBRED

MIDDLE EAST AND AFRICA

CASPIAN
PONY

In 1965 a herd of ponies was discovered
on the southern shores of the Caspian Sea.
Their distinctive appearance bore a
striking resemblance to carvings on the
walls of Persepolis dating back to the fifth
or sixth centuries BC. There had been no
more recent record of these small horses,
known to have been used by the
Mesopotamians 5,000 years ago, but
research confirmed the Caspian pony to
be a direct descendant.

ORIGIN Iran
COLOUR bay, brown,
chestnut or grey
HEIGHT 10–12 hands
PHYSIQUE Arab-type head
on long neck, narrow body
with short back, fine legs,
high-set tail
FEATURES surefooted

CHARACTER gentle, quick-
witted, tractable
PRINCIPAL USES riding,
driving

ANCESTRY

ASIATIC WILD HORSE

BARB
WARMBLOOD

The Barb – from the Barbary Coast of North Africa – is the traditional mount of the Bedouin, and has lived in the region since prehistoric times. The conquering Moors and Turks left Barb stock to found many notable European breeds, including the Andalusian in Spain, and Barbs imported to Britain contributed to the Thoroughbred. Today fewer pure-bred Barbs are left; most having been crossed with Arabs to make them easier to train as riding horses.

ANCESTRY

EUROPEAN WILD STOCK

ORIGIN Algeria and Morocco
COLOUR bay, brown, chestnut, black or grey
HEIGHT 14–15 hands
PHYSIQUE long refined head with straight face, crested neck, flat shoulders, long back, long fine legs, low-set tail

FEATURES frugal and tough
CHARACTER quick-tempered and courageous
PRINCIPAL USES riding, cross-breeding

PERSIAN ARAB
THOROUGHBRED

The Persian Arab is one of the oldest pure Arab lines in the world: bones of a horse excavated in western Iran prove that it lived there long before domestication and that it has changed little since prehistoric times.

ORIGIN Iran

COLOUR grey or bay

HEIGHT 15 hands

PHYSIQUE Arab-type but taller and without the typical "dished" face, elegant compact body

FEATURES larger and less hardy than desert-bred cousin

CHARACTER intelligent, lively and kind

PRINCIPAL USES riding, cross-breeding

ANCESTRY

ASIATIC WILD HORSE

BASUTO
PONY

The Basuto's immediate ancestor, the Cape Horse, was a tough breed which became the cavalry mount of the British army, both in India and in South Africa. Horses left behind in raids on Basutoland deteriorated in quality but became extremely tough, courageous and enduring.

ANCESTRY

ARAB

BARB

THOROUGHBRED

PERSIAN ARAB

ORIGIN South Africa

COLOUR chestnut, bay, brown or grey

HEIGHT 14.2 hands

PHYSIQUE refined head on long neck, straight shoulders, long back, short legs with hard feet

FEATURES very tough and enduring

CHARACTER fearless

PRINCIPAL USES riding, trekking

MANIPUR
PONY

The Manipur is the original polo pony –
the game being played in India on these
fast, manoeuvrable ponies was recorded
as early as the seventh century. The first
British players rode the Manipur, too, but it
has been since superseded by larger,
faster horses.

ORIGIN India
COLOUR most colours
HEIGHT 11–13 hands
PHYSIQUE long head with
broad muzzle, deep chest,
broad deep body on clean
hard legs, high-set tail
FEATURES quick and
manoeuvrable
CHARACTER adaptable and
lively
PRINCIPAL USES riding,
polo, cavalry

ANCESTRY

MONGOLIAN WILD
HORSE

ARAB

BURMA
PONY

For centuries bred by the Shan hill tribes of
eastern Burma, this larger version of the
Indian Manipur is also known as the Shan.
Its strength makes it a good working pony,
but attempts by the British to train it as a
polo pony were not successful.

ORIGIN Burma
COLOUR all colours
HEIGHT 13 hands
PHYSIQUE similar to
Manipur but larger
FEATURES strong hill-pony,
active
CHARACTER adaptable
PRINCIPAL USES all-round
working pony

ANCESTRY

MONGOLIAN WILD
HORSE

ARAB

FAR EAST AND AUSTRALASIA

AUSTRALIAN STOCK HORSE
WARMBLOOD

Until 1971 known as the Waler, which was developed from South African stock crossed with Thoroughbreds, this hardy, agile horse was worked on the cattle stations and served the cavalry regiments in British India.

ORIGIN New South Wales, Australia

COLOUR all colours

HEIGHT 16 hands

PHYSIQUE variable, but Thoroughbred-type with alert head, deep girth, strong back and hindquarters

FEATURES hardy, strong constitution and agile

CHARACTER willing and versatile, a reliable hard worker

PRINCIPAL USES herding, rodeos, riding, competition

ANCESTRY

ARAB

SPANISH

THOROUGHBRED

SUMBA
PONY

A native of a small island in eastern Indonesia, the Sumba is best known as a dancing pony. It is ridden bareback by a small boy and dances, with bells on its knees, to a tom-tom rhythm. Very similar is the Sumbawa.

ORIGIN Sumba, Indonesia

COLOUR dun with dorsal stripe and dark points

HEIGHT 12.2 hands

PHYSIQUE primitive pony-type with heavy head, upright mane and sparse tail

FEATURES specializes as dancing pony

CHARACTER willing, intelligent and tough

PRINCIPAL USES dancing, all-round work pony

ANCESTRY

MONGOLIAN WILD HORSE

TARPAN

AUSTRALIAN PONY
PONY

The foundation stock for this elegant little pony was Arab crossed with Welsh Mountain Pony (most famous one called Grey Light, imported in 1911). By 1929 a specific type had been recognized and a stud book opened.

ANCESTRY

ARAB

WELSH

EXMOOR

SHETLAND PONY

THOROUGHBRED

TIMOR PONY

ORIGIN Australia
COLOUR all colours
HEIGHT 12–14 hands
PHYSIQUE Arab-like head on longish neck, sloping shoulders, deep girth, short back and powerful hindquarters, short legs with hard feet, high-set tail
FEATURES elegant, but enduring and athletic

CHARACTER intelligent and lively
PRINCIPAL USES children's riding pony

B R U M B Y
WARMBLOOD

The Brumby is the wild horse of Australia, descended from riding and packhorses let loose after the gold rush over 100 years ago. "Brumby runners" round up and cull the horses, selling the best as saddle horses.

ORIGIN Australia
COLOUR most colours
HEIGHT variable
PHYSIQUE variable
FEATURES tough and adaptable
CHARACTER alert, wily and intelligent
PRINCIPAL USES too wild for most purposes

ANCESTRY

DOMESTICATED STOCK

SADDLE HORSES

J A V A
PONY

In its native Java, this little pony pulls the *sados*, or two-wheeled taxis, and over the centuries has adapted to hard work in a tropical climate. Similar breeds are to be found on other Indonesian islands: the Timor (of delicate build and very knowing), the Bali (a primitive breed used as a packhorse), the Batak and Gayoc from Sumatra and the Sandalwood, a fast pony from Sumba.

ORIGIN Java
COLOUR most colours
HEIGHT 12.2 hands
PHYSIQUE slightly built but strong pony-type
FEATURES strong and tireless
CHARACTER willing
PRINCIPAL USES driving, all-round work pony

ANCESTRY

TARPAN

ASIATIC WILD HORSE

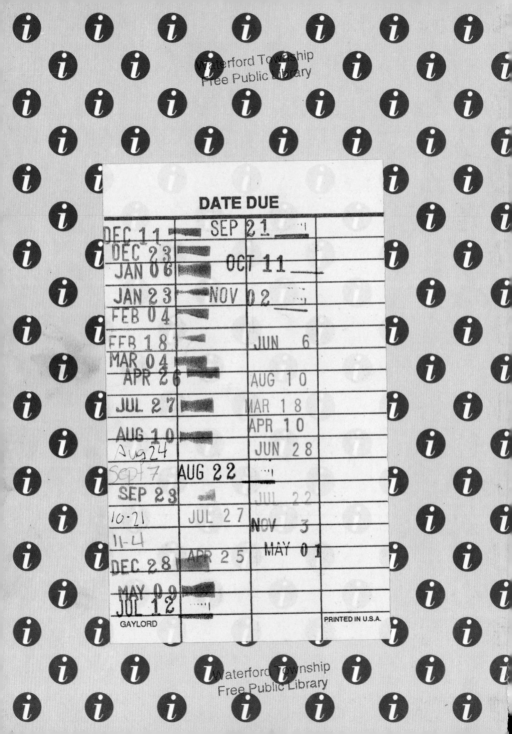

DATE DUE

DEC 11	SEP 21	
DEC 23		
JAN 06	OCT 11	
JAN 23	NOV 02	
FEB 04		
FEB 18	JUN 6	
MAR 04		
APR 26	AUG 10	
JUL 27	MAR 18	
AUG 10	APR 10	
Aug 24	JUN 28	
Sep 7	AUG 22	
SEP 23	JUL 22	
10-21	JUL 27	NOV 3
11-4		MAY 01
DEC 28	APR 25	
MAY 09		
JUL 12		

GAYLORD   PRINTED IN U.S.A.